A NEST OF TIGERS

Finola Holiday

SCRIPTORA

Published in Great Britain in 2023
by
SCRIPTORA

42 Brookside Avenue
Polegate, Eastbourne
East Sussex BN26 6DH

In association with the Society of Women Writers & Journalists
www.swwj.co.uk

ISBN: 978-0-9500591-9-8

Printed and bound by Witley Press Ltd
Hunstanton PE36 6AD
www.witleypress.co.uk

ACKNOWLEDGEMENTS

My thanks are due to the editors of 'South Poetry Magazine' who have enabled my work to appear in more than thirty of their numbers and who have afforded me the privilege of giving me a 'Poet's Profile' in a special issue.

My poems have been extensively published in the 'Downlander' which is the voice of the Downland Poets of Eastbourne. They have also appeared in the 'Ver Poets' publications, 'The Woman Writer', the journal of the Society of Women Writers and Journalists, and in Sussex newspapers and journals.

CONTENTS

PEACOCK EVENING

Pot-bellied yellow fungi
bubble up on the croquet lawn
where the cock-a-hoop peacocks
are slowly feathering down
in the last of the sun.
This is not the time
for strutting their stuff
in front of the small brown
flustering peahens.

Spring was the season
for high-tailing it
through the fine-feathered
sweet talking days
when the peahen hearts
were suddenly ovoid,
their bird brains set
on nest-egging nuptials
under the easy trees.

Now the gold-crested light
is edging away
and a cold wind fingers
a few hang-nail feathers.
Blue iridescence dims,
snake necks wind down –
coil under wings.

Earnley. Sussex.

A NEST OF TIGERS

My grandfather
rode out of the century
on his white horse.
As the December sun
went down for the last time
on the ox-bow river
the swans put on their fine
gold-fingered feathers.

My grandfather
rode out of the Weald
as the old moon went down
for the last time.
His horse's hooves
struck sparks from the stone road
and in the lantern light
the gorse sprigs flowered.

My grandfather
saw the lighted windows
of farmsteads far away
diminish in distance.
No fire-fall galaxies
ripped through the winter velvet
of his sky. No tall bells bruised
the edge of silence.

My grandfather
rode through the quiet cold
to Chanctonbury –
towards the hill-top fires
and the new century.

He never noticed the years
crouching under the hill –
he did not know they held
a nest of tigers.

Sussex. January 1900.

VAN GOGH'S "THE STARRY NIGHT"

A cypress tree, dark as a death-wish
rises against the sky – the peasant village
benighted in its valley huddles down
against a ridge of hills – its hollow steeple
importunes heaven above – a scattered few
casements are still alive with lantern light

and the starry starry night wheels on above them
its spheres on fire, spiralling out of control
and a tiger moon is waxing wild and bright
as if a new god was reshaping heaven –
spinning the careless stars for his delight.

    *   *   *   *   *   *   *   *

A low wall serves as easel for a canvas –
stretched taut with angst and textured with despair,
the palette with its transcendental colours
portrays a radiant other-worldly sphere,
a fire-fall set against the face of darkness –
for time will grant few masterpieces more.

"The Starry Night" was painted only a few months before
Van Gogh's suicide in 1890.

ON FINDING A PRINT OF SIR EDWARD BURNE-JONES' "STUDY FOR THE BRIAR ROSE" IN A CHARITY SHOP

When I came in nobody was kneeling
or staring in wide-eyed wonder
through the girl was clearly among them,
propped by the old shoes and the soft toys.
Unaware, they were turning over
purple curtains, pistachio blouses
not noticing she was breathing
under her frail silk dress.

Spelled in a green reverie
she knelt by the balustrade
of a garden that never was,
the roses of legend round her –
and she, day-dreaming deep,
bethought her a knight rode out
from the wood at the end of the world
to woo her, his love, his lady.

"That will be two ninety-five,"
said the woman behind the till.
"I will give you a bin-liner
to put her in. She has been
here for some time. Now-a-days
no-one has the space – besides
they would not want such a thing
on the sitting-room wall."

FOUND OBJECT

On this wild tide rafts of driftwood
come up the cove – the beached salt-bleached
bones of wrecked craft – worm-holed, old.
Torn from a sea-grave, swung
tide-wise, wave-wide, they ride
a carousel of currents
and arrive, shell-scalloped flotsam –
storm-stuff that the spring tide
casts high and dry –
then runs away to sea.

From this clutter of jetsam,
from this tangle of words
it is possible to find
one verb-grey peerless piece
of drift-wood – one sensuous
gull-winged ghost-rib
of Adam's ilk, the kind
he dreamed to life.

This is the soul-wood of woman,
hollowed out, sea-hallowed,
almost alive and leaning
towards you – the object
of your desire.

Arrange it lovingly
in a low bowl
with a round stone
and one ikebana lily.

Adore it.

LINES FOR A DEAD PRINCESS
(After a painting by Mikhail Nesterov)

We see you wandering
in a dream country,
sleep-walking out of life
eyes slanted shut.
On this, the first day
of your death the forest ways
are sheened with silver
and the awakening wood
is flecked with green.

You stand in the young sun
under the birch-boughs,
your dress of pale brocade
brushing the cowslips,
your locket set with tears
nacreous as pearl, your halo
spun of new gold, an icon
not yet revered.

Beyond the woods a village
lies in the after-light
of long ago, a spire
fingers the sky
its blue dome starred with gold
in a Russia that never was.

Russian Exhibition
Royal Academy
Spring 2008.

WOMAN IS FROM THE MOON

By the dawn wood in winter
he walked, his scarecrow shadow
stretched out on the stubble of snow
as the sun, at its red rising
climbed the bare-limbed trees.

He wore his loneliness –
a hair-shirt next his heart
for even in the ritual night
he found no tenderness
in candle-ends of dream.

And nothing waited beyond
his certainty of returning
to the simple dark before womb was,
to unbeing before the sun
and the burning stars.

Then out of a matrix of mind
she came, a white witch, a moon-charm
into the eye of his longing,
sweet to the touch and the tongue,
soft to his loving.

Though he lives with his fear now
in the new warm world of her
loving him back and yet
expecting the spell's ending
in the snow-blind land of his heart –
knowing that she is woman
from the cold of the moon.

TREES IN WINTER

Briars squat at the wood's margins,
muffled up
in last year's 'Old Man's Beard'.
Planted on open ground
tomorrow's forest
is weathering the winter,
their silhouettes cut sharp
against the sky.
The young trees stand alone
on threadbare grass.
Bereft of leaves and birds
there is no getting together
with the breeze.
They are as quiet
as statues of trees. Bronze torsos
stream with rain. Long limbs
reprise their arabesques.
Perhaps
a fitful sun will come
to spin their shadows.

Soon they will hear the grass
growing again, – a hint of wind
shifting to the south –
the rain suddenly kind.
When the spring touches them
such a tomorrow
will be a time to dance,
a time for frail green fans
to open, begin to wave.

SNOW

Snow falls, the wheel-shafts of the world
clog up. Cogs lock and judder. Fail.
Then silence inches up
and colour spools wind back
to black and white.

The day is other-where. Stepping soft-shoed
the breeze idles, wind-milling the snow,
the morning is fragile, quiet,
after the yesterdays
that rattled through.

The park is shining like a Christmas cake
hard-iced, sun-spun, delicately piped
with a few casual snow-men –
till dusk rubs out their shadows
one by one.

Outside the elm trees ghost, a dog-fox barks
while the night zeros in.
White moths are fluttering –
their cold wings brush my face
with dead kisses.

THAW

Yesterday was wonderland
the turning world
stopped in its tracks.
The lifeless woods
spawned Christmas trees
tinselled with ice, in hedgerows
snowberries grew.
There were cold feathers spread
on angel pavements –
even the cobbled streets
were hushed and holy,
silent with snow.

Today a tribe of snowmen
is facing meltdown
and a world charmed asleep
wakes up to find
the dream was brief.
Yesterday's vestal streets
are brash with slush.
The wind in a torn coat
waits on the corner.
The grass is pricking back
sodden and soiled, the world
is old again and poor.

THE STONES OF CALLANISH

A sky of sorrowful light
broods over the stones,
over the Druid Hill
where the Celts came robed
to greet the solstice.

Touch their sides with your hands,
forms honed by the wind,
smoothed by salt sand
into the shapes of prayer
golden with the old fire
of the earth's core.

They have been standing here,
tall shadows on the peat –
since the beginning.
Before the hermit saints
were washed ashore
they stood at the doors
of knowing – now the stars
candle-light their sleep.

GOING TO COLONSAY

It is too late to go to Colonsay
where the frail light falls softly on the sea,
the ferry boat can take you – but for me
it might as well be half the world away.

I can still see the island in my mind –
the yellow iris shining on the shore,
the bracken clefs that curl from a fern floor,
the waves that spread their lace along the sand.

In June the darkness never quite comes down –
there in the north where the deer call at night
the Summer Isles lie in a long twilight
till the tide swings them back towards the dawn.

In here the nurses come to shake my bed
and bustle round the ward with supper trays,
they chatter of their summer holidays –
in France with Tom or Malaga with Ted.

But I – I long to see the gorse in bloom
beside the sea loch, there on Colonsay
and hear again that single piper play
tunes to take with me to a downstairs room.

BARRA

You promised to bring me
to your island, your sea-land
in the spell of summer.
Where the yellow iris
grows down to the sea
we would be together.

Now, in the long light
I look for your footprints,
your steps alongside mine
by the Celtic sea,
by the shell-spun sand –
but only the Viking wind
with a knife in its teeth
keeps pace with me.

You will never come back
from your forever,
from your hereafter of islands
to walk beside me
even for this one hour
at the ebb of the light
with the tide going out
on the cockle shore.

Outer Hebrides.

SCALPAY (HARRIS)

Weaving the cloth –
the warp and the weft,
hear the click-clack
of the shuttle's song
all the lanterned winter,
all the days of snow.
At your door the sea-loch,
the door your good-man
left long ago
to lie with a merlady
when the grey gales blew –
or so they say.

SUNFLOWERS OF PROVENCE

We flourished here
long before we were famous –
before a mad genius
spattered us on to canvas
and turned our ochre fields
to lunatic landscapes.

Nobody looked at us
before we were logos
and synonyms for sunshine,
before our images
were stamped on shopping bags,
painted on pots.

We were unsuitable
for flower arrangements,
for fireplaces and foyers –
only the children watched us
as we pirouetted
in our green and gold.

We flowered through antique summers,
we were there to see
the lavender harvested,
the vineyards ripening –
under the sundial shadow
of the cypress tree.

BUTTERFLY ON MONT-CANISY

On this thistledown day
your chrysalis opens
and tissue-paper wings
begin to unfold.
The ink is hardly dry
on the art-deco logo
that singles out your species
of butterfly.

As the sun finds you
your hinged wings will begin
their flight checks – fine tuning
that will flitter you into the air
over colts-foot and clover
for wild-flower nectar.

May you survive
the solstice, may your life's day
be the longest, before
you cross a bird's eye
or the wind flails you
out to the sea-shore.

You might find a mate
in the lee of an orchid,
your spinnaker sail
furled in the wind's shade
but live this sun-dance day
for after moonrise
wings will be memories –
torn silks in a grass glade.

Deauville. Midsummer Day.

16

IN MONET'S GARDEN AT GIVERNY

They have painted his bridge 'government green'
in place of the weathered look
it had once – they have reinforced it
for the pilgriming feet.
The bird songs in the green shade
sound just the same although time
has flowed on ahead like the stream.
They have smothered his paths in concrete
to preserve them – though his willows
still reach down for their shadows
among the water lilies –
dark rafts riding at anchor,
floating their coloured candles
on pools of green glass.

Flowers brim over his borders
frail batik silks, brocade reds
run amok in a palette of poppies
and hyacinth blues – clematis,
mignonette, love-in-the mist,
scatter the windfall light.

The yew trees standing together
in pillars of shade remember
how twilight came to the garden
as his eyes dimmed and the canvas
grew sombre – when tiger-lilies
glowered in the dusk and blindness
came in at the gate, when the mist
dropped down on a river flowing
into the dark, forgetting
the water-lilies waiting under the water
for the world to turn, for the sun.

OF THE CISTERCIAN MONKS OF
FONTENAY ABBEY, BEAUNE.

Their water-wheel still turns
but their time has flowed away
with the river – their prayers
long prayed, the night-stair
now left untrodden
by their midnight feet.

Only the nomad sun
sees the bowed shadows
moving across the flag-stones,
passing between the columns
in the abandoned cloister
at the hour of vespers.

Their abbey church stands empty –
stark and austere, possessing
no company of angels
or plaster saints at prayer,
no azure-eyed Madonna
to bestow a blessing.
They feared the artist's palette
could corrupt the soul.

Yet they must have seen
the flush of yellow roses
trailing their careless velvet
over the wall and stood
under the Marian blue
of a summer sky
to glimpse, beyond their grave-grass,
the green hope of heaven.

Fontenay is now a World Heritage site.

DUBLIN DOORWAYS

These long frowning facades
are jewelled with doorways,
dove-tailed feathers of fanlights
wrought black and white,
Georgian, frail.

Generations of polished shoes
passed over these thresholds
and sometimes down-at-heel
pairs of old brogues
bent on intrigue
slipped over the sill.

Intellectual letter-boxes
expected poems
to be pushed through.
Their brassy neighbours
had wire cages inside
lying in wait
for paper tigers.
Thin slits in dark doors
looked for the late post
to bring them love-letters
sprinkled with kisses, inked
with assignations.

MAKING A VEGAN SALAD IN DUBLIN

Sure, I can toss you a salad
in an olive-wood bowl
with never a prawn or a shrimp
or an egg, hard-boiled
for the yoke of a soul
and the lettuces crimped.
I will drizzle olive oil
as extra virgin as the Virgin Queen,
peas will be politically green –
hard enough for a Grimm's princess, cress
pulled from some virtuous bed,
the coleslaw chilled, undressed,
the baby beetroot bled
and tomatoes certainly 'plum'.
Cucumbers fresh from circumcision,
knife-shy, smarting with lemon
will garnish the plate,
the young carrots grated, croutons
cremated – scattered. No capers
for cutting, no red-lipped peppers –
otherwise all of the best
for a fast-day feast.

My forebears were constrained
to share your taste – they once
supped nettle soup, ate dock and dandelion
until their mouths were green, until
the flesh shrank from their bones. The wolf-hounds
died – but that was famine time – aeons ago
and pheasant, venison, oysters all abound
in Erin now.

JOURNEY IN OLD CASTILE

The journey is waiting for you
the horses are saddled, Caballero,
they stand beside their shadows
against the harsh white wall.
In the courtyard the fountain
trembles with tears.

Across the Sierra de Gredos
there is a cloister, Caballero
and here, in a silence of lilies
time has worn out the stone
and jasmine flowers have covered
the sundial's face.

In the high noon of summer
the bulls stand still in the pastures,
there is a hint of thunder
from skies arrowed with swallows.
The poppies shed their silks
before the reaper.

In the first hour of evening
you will cross the shadow of towers.
In holy Toledo, Caballero
the hushed streets are at Vespers
and the soft golden air
is bruised with bells.

POEMA ANDALUZ

With my old cobwebbed heart and my splayed brown feet
I am so little worth that even Death does not want me –
though often he rides this way on his cold stallion
he does not lift me up to his saddle bow.

His hunger is for the young, his arms are spread
to catch them as they fall from the edge of living.
He rides to seek them out, to make them welcome –
lithe-limbed and golden haired, into his kingdom.

If I should enter there I would be brushed aside
to crouch in the doorway wrapped in my old black shawl.

JU-JU DANCE

To belong to Africa
is to be part of the night –
to be one of the twilight people
trapped in the silences
of the empty sky.

There may be a fennec's lair
beyond the circle of fire.
In the space behind the darkness
the small animal winds
whimper all night.

Through incandescent flames
burn the incantations,
the murmurings of magic –
the bundles of charred feathers,
the heart-beats of drums.

To move among the dancers
you will need a disguise.
take up a wooden moon-mask,
hold out a tambourine
jingling with stars.

Fire spirits laugh aloud
as the smoke uncoils, as the feet
stumble and thump and stamp
till the earth quickens its beat
in time to the drums.

Sword blades, sliding on steel
shiver and flicker
and antimony robes
stain the dark skin
with indigo and silver.

The flames lie down to sleep
in a tent of shadow –
in this place the dead will gather
till the gold salamander
eats up the stars.

IMAGES OF AFRICA

The poplar leaves
filter down sunshine.
From skies too bright to bear
clouds of silver balloons
radiate light.

The weaver birds
do yellow aerobatics –
their nests, like circus balls,
teeter on high branches
in a tent of shade.

From the deep sources
under the hills
artesian water spills
and seeps away
into bewildered pools.

Water a million years old
stares at the sky
and breaks into mirrors.
The green parakeets
admire their feathers.

On this unlikely stage
a girl advances
dressed in wild silk.
Blue heads of agapanthus
wilt in the heat.

The wind pulls at her shirt,
his dirty hands
ruffle her hair.
Small droplets of fear
glint on gold skin.

A dust devil
bowls out of nowhere
in a tangle of limbs.
Crickets in concert rasp
bows over strings.

The wind has a cave,
an ugly place to take
the agapanthus girl.
Poplars rattle their leaves
but are too late.

At the rim of the sky
patterns of carrion wings
form and revolve.
Fragments of wild silk lie
on the ground like flowers.

SERENDIPITY

They met at 'thirty thousand' –
slotted in at random
by the airline's computer.
Polite exchanges brought
convivial conversation
then a meeting of minds.

They watched the lighted world
tilt away behind them.
They saw the night flood in
to fill the circling sky
with shoals of stars.

Snug in a silver skin,
cocooned from 'fifty below'
they laughed a little,
explored their coffee cups
for sugar crystals
and raised a glass to drink
a toast to life.

He handed her a pillow
feathered with cloud and soft
as sleep. He could have been
one of the Seven Princes
of Serend.

Dawn broke in another country,
its landscape lying
in grey, after-snow sleep.
Outside the ribboning roadways
were dark with ice.

They humped brief-cases, bags,
focussing out – almost forgetting
to say goodbye.

THE YELLOW CAR

The yellow car
is waiting for you
on the corner lot,
waiting to stun your eyes
like a jazz sunrise.
It will be going home
with you, prepared
to show you how the road
will unwind before you
and ready to lend its wheels
to take your life
faster towards tomorrow.
Inside will be a key
marked 'Freedom'.

Remember there might be
ice on the bridge, remember
the jig-saw corner, the broken culvert –
then go with the yellow car
on the great adventure.
Together you may discover
the cache of gold that lies
in the wood at the end of the world
or find the hidden road
to Shangri-La.

THE FINDING OF MALLORY

The wind whiplashed your back
naked – otherwise left you
almost intact. Only the odd sock
went missing. The love-letter
was still in your pocket, the name-tape
still on your collar.

After the rope broke you took
a little time to die –
clawing the shale, crossing
one boot over the other –
waiting for the cold to bring you
a kind of mercy.

You did not hope for help –
this was a frontier too far
for a cry to cross, you heard
the silence under the wind
and knew an answering shout
could never reach you.

* * * * *

Seventy-five years on
the search-party arrived.
Their orange anoraks
dotted the Himalaya,
their state-of-the-art blue ropes
snaked over the snow.

Their agitated 'phones
cracked open the silences
that had held you in limbo –
a legend, almost a hero
who died incommunicado
quietly in sepia.

Failing to find your camera
they did not stay long
in the Death Zone. They left you
a small homage of stones
and then, before their going,
improvised a prayer.

THAT WAS ON THE EIGER

"Never look down," he said, "for the ground
might spin up to meet you.
Fear is a vortex that could suck you in
so focus on finger-holds, take care
of the slack in your rope.
Hang on, curl your toes in a crack,
lean in to the slope."

"Never let go," he said, "you could drag
the next man with you, clip on
to the face, get your breath.
As to falling a thousand feet –
arms flailing like wings
with the glacier gleaming beneath –
leave that to the falcons."

"Stay with the crack," he said, "this pitch
is for birds – only remember
the irreversible traverse
is on the Eiger, not here –
so go for the top.
Before the cloud comes over
we can all be up."

    *   *   *   *   *

"Never give in," he said. "Stay awake –
tough luck that we had to abandon
the rucksacks – no one could know
the weather would break.
Dream up a bar of chocolate
and be glad of the pain in your feet –
it means you can feel them still.
Never lie down in the snow
sleep can kill."

"Never push your luck," he said. "When it's out.
Only a fly could crawl back
down that pitch in the dark – we should rope
to the face, wait out the night.
No, this was never the place
they called 'Death Bivouac',
that was on the Eiger. Remember
the wind could still drop.
Try not... to give up..."

BRIGHTON SUNSET

Over the dead pier, that heap of iron bones,
bones that will not lie down in their sea-grave,
over the waves where the red winter sun
floats for a moment and is gone, they come –
a weft of wings, a tapestry of birds
unfurls against the back-drop of the sky –
synchronised fliers with a thousand wings,
performers in some starling Cirque du Soleil
they soar in perfect arcs and loops and rings
in tight formation, feathering the wind
then dive towards the shore-line – pulling out
to vanish in the nowhere of the night.

THE ROCKIES

These peaks have never known
a dress of grass,
the small blue lamps
of gentians, the wild silks
of old world flowers.
Their ragged faces bear
the griefs of ice
and on their altars burn
the candled stars –
faint flames to intercede
with their cold sun
to wake their waterfalls,
make their streams flow.

Like caryatids they bear
great domes of snow
that sunset's alchemy
turns to fool's gold.
Their feet are locked in lakes –
wilds where the wind goes
softly along their shores
a whetted hunting knife
clasped in his teeth.
The only watcher there
has the cold eyes of a wolf
and a wolf's stare.

THE FALLS AT ELBOW RIVER

The water makes a white fist
to jostle aside the stones.
The river is in a hurry
having a valley to carve
and mountains to move
with only a few million years
to get it done.

The breeze is beginning
to finger the birch leaves –
turning them over gently,
smoothing the silver
but the left wind at my shoulder
is speaking of winter –
when no rivers run.

There is little time now
for that urgency of water
to leap over the strata
through a hoop of rainbows.
That bull-buffalo roar
will fade to a whimper
in the deeps of winter.

On a night of 'thirty below'
the cold will zero in
and a stream tongued with ice
will choke in its flow
stumbling over the boulders,
falling to its death –
strewing the precipice
with broken crystals.

PAINTING THE MARA

Before earth turns towards
the dawn, before
the sky remembers blueness
and the last stars
still pin-prick through your canvas
this is the moment for you
to pencil in the shoreline,
fill in a stand of pine trees
with a stub of charcoal.
The lake is an onyx mirror
where a single brushstroke
will leave a trace of opal
under the glass.
You can drag a soft wash
of colour over your sky-scape,
add in a touch of crimson
and cerulean blue.
You may lighten the leaves
of the background poplars
but save a little darkness
to paint their shadows.
The minute before sunrise
you can splash on yellow,
transpose the sepia landscape
with a flood of colour.
As the light swamps your palette
choose lapis lazuli
it will deepen the water,
fill your lake with sky.

British Columbia, Canada.

35

LULLABY FOR A CHILD BORN
IN THE CANADIAN ARCTIC

In the landscape of love
where you were made
the sun danced and the spring rain
fell on my valley.
You rocked in the womb's world,
in the lake of my life
till the seasons turned
and you were born.

    *   *   *   *   *

In your cotton-wool world
sleep now, blue-eyed child –
outside the wilderness
is burdened with snow.
Sleep as a kitten curled
with her kindred kind
for beyond the window
it is twenty, twenty below.

Sleep safely in your rose warmth
as the pine logs flare,
out there the timber wolves
lope through the snow
and the small furred friars
are burrowed asleep
for outside in the steel air
it is thirty, thirty below.

Sleep as your cradle rocks
to the beat of my blood –
the white fox died in the wild
to give you a hood,
sleep as the mercury falls –
in the silence of frost
take my breast for your pillow
at forty, forty below.

In your swaddling of swansdown
my dear lie soft and warm
for the Catcher of Dreams will come
tip-toe to your bed
to drive the nightmares away
with his feathered web
to graze in the fields of snow
at fifty, fifty below.

THE MAP

You held the map of our life over your knees,
creased at the cross-roads, split on the valley floor.
Always the pages rustled as we journeyed
through frontiers to the hinterlands of love.
It guided us across old-master landscapes,
along roads painted with poplars and took us
to autumn orchards red with peasant apples
and almond groves in a confetti spring.
The map, spread out, led us to hidden places –
an abbey transept where a stained-glass sunset
spilled on your dress, and where an oriole window
made you a halo. Outside the casual wind
swept a strand of your hair across my face.

Now the map of our life is set aside –
rolled up and out of use. Lacking direction
I go now in silence among rivers,
pass under willow shade, almost forgetting
how once I walked in the desiring sun.
My thoughts, like the black swans that glide down-stream
drift out into the dark. The evening wind
still trembles at the memory of your voice.

SAHARA

At dawn they crawl
under the dead truck
as the sun burns round
eating the shadow, leaving
no place to hide.

At night the rocks
creep closer to them –
deep-cowled and robed in shadow,
impatient to intone
a requiem.

All day they dream of water,
of dripping taps, of streams,
of deep cold wells.
Out there mirages shimmer
with long blue lakes.

Specks of burnt paper – vultures
circle the sky, they know
there is no water. Soon
they will drop down and leave
a carrion shroud.

Another night and the moon
spins a gold coin
round the hours to sunrise.
Thirst rasps, lips parch
their last prayer prayed
for water.

In Guezzam – Southern Sahara
1952

OVERFLOW

The sky is underfoot,
it has covered the fields
with grey glass, with polished light.
We wade through the reflection
of an afternoon.

In June the river drifted
sleep-walking through the meadows,
counting its sheep
with the sky overhead
spinning its clouds.

Now the lush fields are changed
into a set designed
for 'Swan Lake', the corps de ballet
glides quietly across
the flood-lit sky.

A brood of cygnets goes
white water rafting
under the stone arches
of the bridge. The torrent takes them
careening by.

The ewes have departed –
long sheep-dogged away
to safely graze. The empty mirror
waits for the frost to turn
the glass to ice.

THE LANDLADY

"Yes, he can stay with you again if he must
although I find it hard to comprehend
how you can shoehorn two people
into that sardine tin of a room of yours –
but I must keep such notions to myself.

You should be aware as far as I am concerned
sleep is a rare guest who comes only
in the small quiet hours. When I retire
the cat on my quilt speaks seldom, the radio
dispenses pillow-talk in a stage whisper.

You may not realise it but your giggle
comes through the wall like a hot knife through butter
round about 3 am. The wall paper
begins to peel and a few flakes of stucco
fall from the ceiling. Sleep is unthinkable.

I do not want love-making in the next room,
happiness leaking through the plaster-board
unsettles me and opens the old wounds
the gaps in the years, the cracks in the façade –
my life is jerry-built, the walls are thin.

So if he comes to stay with you again
you must giggle in whispers – I like to lie awake
in a quiet house so I can hear the wind
trying the doors and know I am secure
with no one to rebuke my solitude."

LOVE IN THE TIME OF 'TINDER'

They met in the park – or rather
she was in the park and he
on a lunch-break scrolling through
desirable images. They met
in the flesh – did not think to enquire
into commitments, raising a glass
to fortune, starting a wild-fire
that swept through their heartland, left them
moonscaped by morning.

THE DARLINGS

Their darlings are so young and beautiful
and always blonde – those macho older men
won them with such articulate aplomb
to prove themselves so wholly adequate.
They take such pride in setting them among
the Chinese porcelain and the Georgian chairs.
They like to see them with the Labradors –
darlings look marvellous in four-by-fours.

And outdoors, darlings always look so good,
as if the wind has just blow-dried their hair,
as if the tide had brought the pearls they wear –
oysters are 'en rapport' with caviar.
They are not fazed by thoughts of widowhood
nor fears of that incipient heart attack –
they hold the credit-cards, the Will is there
and darlings look so ravishing in black.

PUB LUNCH

His person overflowed
the table and chair.
Owl-faced and old
he carped unceasingly
at his blue-rinsed women.
Procrastinating long
he chose the dressed crab
but ignored the lettuce
as it lay before him
like a green grace.
As he poured the tomato ketchup
into his gin
he said he would not care
to come here again.

WINTER SAIL

The frost has starched your sails, it is low-water
in your life – the lake
is winter-dry.
On the shore the fishermen talk of the killer pike
that swarm away.

There is a small wind with ice in its arc
waiting to stalk your sails
waiting to fly
you into the folklore of fisherman's tales
keel-deep in the sky.

Wave-patterns the wind writes on the water
with its quill feathers
blur under your hull.
The fishermen leave their lines and watch together
for your slim sail.

The lake is dark but on the flight-path overhead
at about thirty thousand
there is still sun
but golden sky-script falters on the wind –
"Come in, Number One."

BEFORE THE SNOW

Before the snow
feathers your eyes
with its designer geometry,
before the diamond-down
sets crystal coronets
above your brow,
before the frost-flowers thread
their silver filigree
over your limbs –
there is a moment now,
a time when you may still
look softly on me.

I know that winter
will be forever –
with the hands of the coachman numb
and imagine the horses
dressed in their mourning plumes –
and the frost on their breath.

Remember there will be
no loving where they go –
only the iron-bound earth
and the quietness
of the fallen snow.

THE DOOR TO THE DARK

There is no handle
on the door into the dark.
Someone on the other side
must answer your knock.
You will enter without a lamp
or a canary. Be aware
that moon-rise will not occur,
that the stars will have retreated
behind the night, that the ritual
of sunrise has fallen out of use.

You will feel the flicker
of bat-wing against your cheek
and that sound of water
is the unquiet spirit of a river
wandering in the underworld.
Tears drop on your face – the rocks
build their sad stalactites.
Stretch your arms into the dark
as a blind man might – perhaps
someone will take your hand.